# Giant Leaps

# Space Shuttles

## Stuart A. Kallen

ABDO & Daughters
PUBLISHING

Published by Abdo & Daughters, 4940 Viking Dr., Suite 622, Edina, MN 55435.

Copyright ©1996 by Abdo Consulting Group, Inc., Pentagon Tower, P.O. Box 36036, Minneapolis, Minnesota 55435. International copyrights reserved in all countries. No part of this book may be reproduced in any form without written permission from the publisher. Printed in the United States.

**Cover Photos by:** Archive Photos
**Inside Photos**
Archive Photos: pp. 7, 15, 19, 21, 23, 24, 28
AP/Wide World Photos: pp. 4-5, 18
Bettmann: pp. 9, 11, 16, 25, 27

## Edited by Bob Italia

**Library of Congress Cataloging–in–Publication Data**
Kallen, Stuart A., 1955–
    Space shuttles / by Stuart A. Kallen
    p. cm. — (Giant leaps)
Includes bibliographical references and index.
    Summary: Describes the physical characteristics of space shuttles and life aboard them, and provides a history of the NASA space shuttle program.
    ISBN 1-56239-569-6
    1. Space shuttles—Juvenile literature. 2. Space Shuttle Program (U.S.)—Juvenile literature. [1. Space shuttles. 2. Space flight.] I. Title. II. Series.
    TL795.5.K35  1996
    629.44'1'0973—dc20                                    95-39015
                                                          CIP
                                                          AC

# CONTENTS

Space Shuttles ........................................................ 5

What Goes Up, Must Come Down ........................... 6

What's In A Space Shuttle? ..................................... 8

Space Transport ..................................................... 10

Life On A Space Shuttle ......................................... 11

Spacelab ................................................................. 13

*Enterprise* And *Columbia* ...................................... 14

Tragedy Over Cape Canaveral ............................... 16

Return To Space ..................................................... 20

The Trouble With Hubble ....................................... 22

The Handshake In Orbit ......................................... 26

Final Word .............................................................. 28

Glossary ................................................................. 29

Bibliography ........................................................... 31

Index ...................................................................... 32

# SPACE SHUTTLES

PEOPLE ON EARTH HAVE always dreamed of flying to other planets. In the 1940s, science fiction writers imagined people boarding a rocketship that looked like an airplane. The craft would soar off into space, land on other planets, then fly back to earth. One such story, which was published in a magazine in 1947, had the headline, "All Aboard for the Moon!" Underneath, the story said, "The rocketship will leave at midnight. Back to earth for a late breakfast. Round-trip tickets only."

Such a dream never came to be. But it may someday be possible because of the Space Shuttle.

*This page:* The *Space Shuttle Columbia* rides a crest of flame as it roars into orbit.

# WHAT GOES UP, MUST COME DOWN

There is an old saying that says, "What goes up must come down." This is especially true when applied to the space program. In the early days of spaceflight, expensive rockets were used to put a tiny capsule into orbit. A few people rode in the capsule. Stage by stage, the booster segments fell away during the launch as their fuel ran out. The spacecraft—as big as a delivery van—went into orbit around the earth. Then the 320-foot-long (98-meter-long), multi-stage rocket crashed down into the ocean. It became instant space junk.

During space orbit and trips to the moon, billions of dollars worth of complicated hardware either fell uselessly to the ground or was left in outer space. Valued in today's dollars, the United States abandoned about $300 billion worth of machinery in space. And that was only on the Apollo moon-landing missions. The earlier Mercury and Gemini missions also added to that total.

After the last moon landing in 1973, America's space agency, NASA (National Aeronautics and Space Administration), was told to cut costs. At the time, the American economy was in bad shape. Moon landings no longer were affordable. NASA put aside its plan to send a manned mission to Mars. Instead, they developed the space station *Skylab*. It was the dream of NASA engineers to ferry people and supplies back and forth to *Skylab* with a reusable spacecraft. The Space Shuttle Transportation System (SSTS), or Space Shuttle, was born.

After years of expensive "throwaway" multi-stage rockets, the answer to the waste was a "single stage to orbit" rocket. It was a spacecraft that carried everything it needed to get into orbit. It would do its work and return safely. Nothing would be thrown away or left behind.

*Right:* The *Space Shuttle Endeavour,* part of a new generation of American space vehicles.

# WHAT'S IN A SPACE SHUTTLE?

The Space Shuttle is the first reusable spacecraft. Every other space vehicle was designed for only one flight. The Space Shuttle also can deliver cargo to space and bring it back. Because of its unique design, the Space Shuttle can serve as:

1. A launch vehicle.

2. A platform for scientific laboratories.

3. An orbiting service center for satellites.

4. A return carrier for spacecraft that had been in orbit.

In short, the Space Shuttle is a space "truck" that can carry cargo to and from space.

There are three main sections of a Space Shuttle. The first is the orbiter, which houses the crew and the cargo. The orbiter circles the earth and then returns to a landing strip. The orbiter can hold up to seven people. Two of these people are the mission commander and the copilot. The rest are technical and scientific experts. The orbiter has steering engines but no motor. It is a glider when it

lands on earth at 250 miles (402 kilometers) per hour—twice as fast as a jet airplane.

The second part of a Space Shuttle is a huge tank called the external tank (ET). The orbiter is piggy-backed into space on the ET. It is 154 feet (47 meters) long, and 27 feet (8 meters) in diameter. The ET is filled with liquid hydrogen and liquid oxygen. These chemicals fuel the rocket engines on the rear of the orbiter during liftoff.

The third part of the Space Shuttle are large cylinders called solid rocket boosters (SRB). They are on each side of the ET. They are filled with solid fuel and propel the Space Shuttle during the first two minutes of flight.

It is the SRBs and the extra fuel from the huge ET that generate enough energy to lift the Shuttle into space. These are the largest solid fuel rocket boosters ever flown— 149 feet (45 meters) long and 12 feet (3.7 meters) in diameter. They are also the first designed for reuse.

When they are empty, the SRBs separate from the orbiter and fall by parachute into the ocean. They are then picked up and refilled to help lift another orbiter into space. The ET is the only part that is not reusable. It falls off later and is destroyed by heat and friction as it falls back through the earth's atmosphere.

The orbiter is the main part of the Space Shuttle. It is designed to last for 100 spaceflights. This winged vehicle is part spacecraft, part aircraft. It is as big as a DC-9 jet airplane.

The front section of the Space Shuttle is divided into three floors called the flight deck, the mid-deck, and the lower deck. The flight deck contains the pilot and commander's seats. From the flight deck, the crew controls the flight and orbit of the Shuttle. Windows allow the crew to take pictures in space. Mid-deck is where the crew lives. There are sleep stations, food lockers, bathrooms, and storage lockers. More storage is located in the lower deck. Hydrogen and oxygen are combined in fuel cells to generate electricity and water.

The long middle part of the Shuttle is called the payload bay. Whatever goes in this area is the reason for the mission. It "pays" for the flight. It

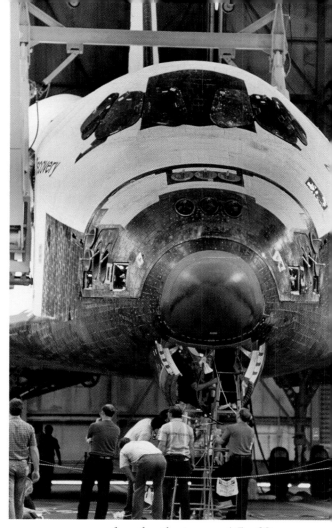

can carry payloads that are 15x60 feet (4.5x18 meters). Some of the payloads on the Shuttle are television satellites and Spacelab laboratories. On top of the payload bay are two large doors. They may be opened to launch a satellite into orbit.

*Above:* Engineers in the vehicle assembly building make sure the nose landing gear of the orbiter *Discovery* is working properly before attaching the solid rocket boosters.

Behind the payload bay are the three engines that propel the orbiter during launch. They are called the Space Shuttle main engines (SSMEs). They are the most advanced liquid-fuel rocket engines ever built. They burn liquid hydrogen and liquid oxygen under high pressure to create as much thrust as possible. Each SSME has a thrust rate of 375,000 pounds (1.6 million newtons). The propellant for these engines is in the external tank.

Located by the engines at the rear of the Shuttle is the orbital maneuvering system (OMS). These engines are used to steer the Shuttle when it is in orbit.

When the Space Shuttle lands, computers pick the exact spot for it to enter the earth's atmosphere. The OMS engines fire to slow the orbiter enough so that the earth's gravity begins to pull it in. Gravity gently pulls the Shuttle down to earth. The orbiter gets extremely hot because of the friction of the atmosphere. The Shuttle is flown by computer and glides unpowered as it lands on a runway.

# SPACE TRANSPORT

The Space Shuttle is an amazing flying machine. But it does not operate alone. It is part of the Space Transportation System (STS). The Space Shuttle is the backbone of the system.

Most communications satellites orbit the earth at a distance of 22,300 miles (35,900 kilometers). But the Space Shuttle only goes to 690 miles (1,100 kilometers). The Space Shuttle delivers satellites to a low orbit. Then a rocket motor attached to the satellite boosts it to a higher orbit. These rocket motors are also part of the STS.

In addition, the STS includes ground facilities where the Shuttle is built, launched, and recovered. Together the STS provides an efficient, economical way to launch all types of satellites. These also include scientific, planetary, or military satellites. The Shuttle also can retrieve some satellites and bring them back to earth for repair.

# LIFE ON A SPACE SHUTTLE

Flying to and from space in a Space Shuttle is easier than in the early years of spaceflight. There is less pressure on takeoffs and landings. For this reason, almost anyone in good health can fly aboard the Shuttle. They do not have to be experienced jet pilots like the early astronauts were.

The first thing Shuttle astronauts do is remove their heavy 90 pound (40.8 kilogram) space suits. This can take a very long time in the zero gravity of space.

Since the astronauts are usually in orbit for only one week, they must

*Below:* The first American woman to walk in space, astronaut Kathryn Sullivan, looks through the window of the *Space Shuttle Challenger.*

work quickly. The first day they activate the Shuttle's systems: lights, communications, air pressure, power, and the bathroom. About two hours after launch, they open the payload bay doors to help release the heat built up in the bay since launch. The doors stay open the whole mission. When the doors face into the sun, the temperature outside the Shuttle may be 300 degrees Fahrenheit (148 degrees Celsius). When the doors face away from the sun into dark, cold space, the temperature may be 300 degrees Fahrenheit below zero. The orbiter rolls to keep an even temperature inside.

Once housekeeping is done, astronauts begin work on their experiments. They study such things as space medicine and industrial processes. They use cameras and videotape recorders to record scientific data. Astronauts must relay long sets of mathematical readings back to earth. Because they are working in such a small space, tools like microscopes must be assembled each time they are used, and then taken apart. Lights are set up for photographs. Seeds are planted. The Shuttle can be a very noisy place when some of the big machinery is running.

The bodies of the astronauts must adjust to zero gravity. Their hearts change shape. Blood returns from the lower body to the heart more easily than it does on earth. This floods the upper body with more blood than is needed. The body adapts by ridding excess fluid through the kidneys. The heart muscle shrinks.

Of course astronauts must eat in space. When scientists first planned spaceflight, they weren't even sure a human could swallow food in zero gravity. The first astronauts ate freeze-dried food cut into cubes. Later, astronauts had food coated in gelatin to keep it from crumbling. Still, they were cold meals. Later, astronauts could inject water into the dried food to pump it up. By the 1969 Apollo moonlanding, astronauts had hot water aboard their spacecraft, which allowed them to have hot food.

Shuttle astronauts dine on shrimp cocktail, tortillas with peanut butter, cheese spreads, or chicken dishes. They also eat candy, snacks, relish, cookies, apples, carrots, and bananas. In all, there are 75 kinds of food and 20 kinds of beverages.

Astronauts must be very careful to keep their food from floating away. Loose food can be hazardous when in zero gravity. It can get in people's eyes, ears, or noses. It also can contaminate experiments or get in critical electrical circuits.

There is no day or night on the Space Shuttle. Each time they circle the earth, the crew sees 45 minutes of daylight and 45 minutes of darkness. The crew divides up sleeping into two shifts, the red (night) shift and the blue (day) shift. It must be done this way because there are only four beds on the Shuttle.

Sleeping in zero gravity is hard. Astronauts must strap on pillows to keep them from bumping into the walls of the sleep compartment.

# SPACELAB

Scientists have tried to perfect a reusable rocketship for decades. But the first three-section Shuttle, like those used today, was approved by President Richard Nixon on January 5, 1972. NASA estimated the cost at $2.6 billion over 6 years. Contracts to build the Shuttle were awarded to aerospace companies Rockwell International, Martin Marietta, McDonnell Douglas, and Thiokol Chemical Corporation. The Shuttle was designed to service space stations, but none existed at the time. It was to be an all-purpose space truck—with nowhere to go.

Besides being a space truck, the Shuttle was projected as a means to begin industrial production in space. Earlier experiments had shown that zero gravity conditions provided a good environment for manufacturing precision substances. These included drugs, metals, and high-purity crystals for electronic components.

Since the United States could not afford a space workshop, NASA became partners with the European Space Agency (ESA). On August 14, 1973, 14 nations put together $500 million to build Spacelab.

Spacelab is a two-sectioned system. One section is a workshop. The other section is a flat place where scientific instruments may be mounted. Spacelab carries six astronauts. The countries that contributed to Spacelab were Austria, Belgium, Denmark, France, West Germany, Italy, the Netherlands, Spain, Switzerland, and the United Kingdom. The first flight of Spacelab was achieved in November 1983.

# ENTERPRISE
# AND *COLUMBIA*

The first Space Shuttle orbiter was called the *Enterprise*. It got its name after 100,000 fans of the TV show "Star Trek" wrote to NASA asking that the name be used. President Gerald Ford decided to use the name. NASA didn't like it, wanting to name the orbiter *Constitution* in honor of America's 200th birthday in 1976.

The first tests, with no astronauts aboard, began in February 1977. Early tests were done with the orbiter firmly attached to the back of a Boeing 747 jet airplane. The first flight with people aboard occurred on August 12, 1977, when astronauts Fred W. Haise and C. Gordon Fullerton flew the 75-ton (68.4-metric-ton) glider around a course to a perfect landing. They had separated from the 747 at 22,800 feet (6,950 meters). This was the heaviest object ever to fly without a motor. Haise and Fullerton were amazed. They said the orbiter flew like a jet fighter.

After more months of tests on the ground, the *Enterprise* was rolled out to a launch pad at Kennedy Space Center. It was joined with the external tank and the solid rocket boosters on the launch platform. The four pieces together weighed 11 million pounds (4.9 million kilograms). It was set up on the launch pad and remained there for thousands of visitors to admire. The *Enterprise* never flew again.

When first started in 1972, NASA planned to fly the first Shuttle into space by 1978. A series of engine and heat shield problems kept pushing the date back. But on April 12, 1981, the orbiter *Columbia* rose from the launch pad at Cape Canaveral. The booster and ET separation went off without a hitch. The SRBs were recovered in good condition about 151 miles (243 kilometers) away. The OMS worked well and the *Columbia* was soon in orbit around the earth.

*Columbia's* commander was John W. Young and its pilot was Captain Robert L. Crippen. *Columbia* made a safe reentry on April 14, touching

down at Edwards Air Force Base in California. It had flown 55 hours and 22 minutes. The next three flights of *Columbia* were research and development missions flown by two-man crews.

The first operational mission was on November 11-16, 1982, when *Columbia* deployed two commercial communications satellites into earth orbit. The scientists on board produced latex beads to be used in medicine to carry medication to cancerous tumors.

*Above:* The *Space Shuttle Columbia* sits on the launch pad at dawn, waiting to blastoff into orbit.

# TRAGEDY OVER CAPE CANAVERAL

The first flight of orbiter *Challenger* was April 4-9, 1983. It carried a four-person crew and deployed a satellite. *Challenger's* second flight, from June 18-24, 1983, carried Dr. Sally K. Ride, the first American woman to fly in space. Ride was the third woman to ever visit space; the others were from the Soviet Union.

Ride was a physicist, and among the large number of astronauts recruited by NASA in the early 1980s. A few months later, another *Challenger* flight took Guion S. Bluford, Jr. into space from August 30 to September 5, 1983. Bluford was the first African-American astronaut to travel into space.

The *Challenger* flight on November 28-December 8, 1983, put the Spacelab into orbit. Spacelab carried 72 experiments in atmospheric physics, earth observations, space medicine, physics, solar physics, and astronomy.

Ride became the first woman to travel in space two times. Her second flight on the *Challenger* was on October 5-13, 1984.

The Space Shuttle missions and the *Challenger* seemed a perfect setup. Besides the *Columbia* and the *Challenger,* two other orbiters, *Discovery* and *Atlantis,* also flew several missions.

Mission after mission roared into space, deposited satellites and conducted experiments. Those satellites were changing things on earth. Telephone communications, TV broadcasts, and computer communications were improved dramatically. Satellites were also deployed for weather observation, earth, moon, and sun observation, and top-secret military applications.

January 28, 1986, was going to be a silver anniversary for the Space Shuttle program—the 25th flight. It was a bright and clear morning at Cape Canaveral. *Challenger* was to lift a satellite called the Tracking and

Data Relay Satellite (TDRS), and send it into orbit around the earth. Built at a cost of $100 million, the TDRS would relay information from other satellites back to earth. The *Challenger* was also to launch a free-flying astronomy module to study Comet Halley.

Up on the flight deck, seven crew members were strapped into their seats. They were: Francis R. Scobee, commander; Michael J. Smith, pilot; Judith A. Resnick, mission specialist (the second American woman in

*Above:* The crew of the doomed *Space Shuttle Challenger.* *Front row, left to right:* Michael J. Smith, Francis R. (Dick) Scobee, and Ronald E. McNair. *Back row, left to right:* Ellison S. Onizuka, school teacher Sharon Christa McAuliffe, Gregory B. Jarvis, and Judith A. Resnik.

space); Ellison S. Onizuka, mission specialist; Ronald E. McNair, mission specialist; Gregory B. Jarvis, payload specialist; and Sharon Christa McAuliffe, a New Hampshire school teacher and the first Space Shuttle passenger in NASA's Teacher in Space program.

McAuliffe planned to teach lessons to school children on earth during live TV transmissions from space. McAuliffe was the best-known crew member. She had won the honor to teach from space over 11,146 other teachers. She was 37 years old.

As usual, millions of TV viewers were tuned in to watch the launch of the *Challenger.* Pupils in classrooms

across the nation took special notice because of McAuliffe.

The launch took place at 11:38 a.m. It seemed to go smoothly at first. When *Challenger* reached an altitude of 47,000 feet (14,325 meters) it was traveling at 1,800 feet (548 meters) per second. Then a small flame brought disaster.

The flame appeared to erupt from the rocket booster near the external tank's right side. Fifteen seconds later, there was a huge explosion as 500,000 gallons (1,892,500 liters) of rocket fuel blew up. *Challenger* was blown to bits. The two solid rocket boosters were sent zig-zagging wildly through the air. America was left staring in horror.

Later, it was revealed that an O-ring that kept the fuel sealed within one of the solid rocket boosters had failed. The flame from the SRB acted like a blowtorch, setting off the explosion of the larger external tank. The tragedy marked the greatest loss of life ever suffered in the history of American space exploration.

On June 13, 1986, President Ronald Reagan ordered NASA to redesign the solid rocket boosters of the Space Shuttle. Over the next several years, 400 changes were made to the entire Shuttle, including the boosters.

*Above:* The *Challenger* explosion on January 28, 1986. The two plumes of smoke coming out of the larger explosion-cloud are the solid rocket boosters.

*Left, facing page:* This picture shows the breakup of the *Challenger* 78 seconds after liftoff. The top arrow shows the Shuttle's left wing. The center arrow shows the Shuttle's main engine. The bottom arrow shows the Shuttle's forward fuselage.

# RETURN
# TO SPACE

The *Challenger* explosion shook the entire country. Many people thought that the Shuttle would never fly again. But after a careful review of Shuttle systems, NASA was ready to try again. On September 29, 1988, more than two and a half years after the *Challenger* disaster, NASA launched the *Discovery*. Crew members assigned to the mission included Commander Frederick H. Hauck, pilot Richard O. Covey, John H. Lounge, David C. Hilmers, and George D. Nelson. The crew deployed another TDRS like the one lost in the *Challenger* accident.

The *Discovery* and *Atlantis* continued to fly dozens of missions. In 1989, *Atlantis* placed the first planetary observatory in space—the *Magellan* radar imaging spacecraft. *Magellan* was carried into low earth orbit and boosted by a two-stage rocket. *Magellan* launched off toward the planet Venus, where it sent beautiful pictures back to earth many months later.

On May 10, 1989, President George Bush announced the name for a new Shuttle orbiter—*Endeavour*. The name was voted the most popular in a contest entered by more than 71,000 students across America. *Endeavour* was the name of a sailing ship used by Captain James Cook, an 18th-century British explorer. Cook explored the South Pacific in the *Endeavour* from 1768 to 1772. He later sailed around the entire globe in the ship. (Although the American spelling of the word is Endeavor, President Bush chose the original English spelling.) *Endeavour* launched on its first flight on May 16, 1992.

---

*Right:* The *Space Shuttle Endeavour* lifts off from the Kennedy Space Center.

# THE TROUBLE WITH HUBBLE

On April 25, 1990, NASA launched the $1.6 billion Hubble Space Telescope. Hubble was equipped with a 7-foot-8-inch (2.3-meter) mirror that would allow observation of very distant stars. It was to have 50 times more power than any telescope on earth.

Unfortunately, Hubble was in trouble from the start. The main problem was that the giant mirror was never focused properly. Instead of bringing in brilliant pictures of distant galaxies, all of Hubble's images were a blur. There were also problems with electronic systems, stabilizer systems, and solar-energy panels. Perhaps the biggest mistake was that none of these problems was discovered until the giant telescope was already in space.

For more than three years, NASA suffered public relations woes as Congress used the mistakes as an excuse to cut funding. Hubble was just one more blunder after the 1986 *Challenger* explosion. But in January 1994, NASA was able to use the *Space Shuttle Endeavour* to fix Hubble.

The mission was a tough one. It would require a crew of seven to fly up next to the Hubble in space. Then two pairs of astronauts would go on five spacewalks of six hours each, which would set a record. The astronauts would focus the mirror and do many other complicated repairs outside a spacecraft orbiting the earth at 17,000 miles an hour (27,353 kilometers per hour). The task required a repair kit consisting of 280 tools and 15,000 pounds (6,810 kilograms) of equipment.

Because of the difficulty of working in space, *Time* magazine said the repair work would "be something like weaving baskets while wearing boxing gloves in a

*Right: Space Shuttle Discovery* rises from the launch pad.

weightless environment." It was considered the toughest task faced by NASA since the moon landings. Success was not insured.

With so much at stake, NASA assembled the best seven-person crew available. Dr. Story Musgrave, the payload commander, had seven college degrees and had flown on four previous Shuttle flights. The Shuttle commander, Richard Covey, was a former fighter pilot with 339 combat missions. He also was the man picked in 1988 to fly the first Shuttle after the *Challenger* disaster. Navy pilot Kenneth Bowersox, who would help Covey maneuver the *Endeavour* into orbit with the

---

*Below:* Astronaut Jeffrey Hoffman displays tools used in the five spacewalks to fix the Hubble Space Telescope.

Hubble, had made more than 300 landings of fighter planes on the rolling decks of aircraft carriers. The four astronauts who would make the difficult spacewalks and repairs were Musgrave, Jeffrey Hoffman, Thomas Akers, and Kathryn Thornton. All of them were experienced spacewalkers. Thornton, a mother of five and a nuclear physicist, helped repair a communications satellite in 1992.

To train for the repair mission, the crew trained on 70-hour work weeks for 10 months. NASA tripled the amount of time spent training on spacewalks. The astronauts spent 400 hours working under water to imitate the conditions in outer space. They stayed under water for seven hours at a time and rehearsed every step of the repair job. The astronauts also worked in a chamber that was chilled to 300 degrees below zero Fahrenheit (148 degrees below zero Celsius). During one session, Musgrave got frostbite on his fingers. NASA was forced to improve the space suits and put extra covering on the gloves.

On January 7, 1993, the *Endeavour* blasted off in a perfect launch from Cape Canaveral. Within days, the *Endeavour* closed the 6,700-mile (10,780-kilometer) gap between it and the Hubble. Covey steered the *Endeavour* within 35 feet (10.7 meters) of the telescope. Astronauts used a robot arm to grab the 25,000-pound (11,350-kilogram) telescope. They pulled it into the payload bay, where some of the repairs would be made. Covey radioed back to earth, "*Endeavour* has a firm handshake with Mr. Hubble's telescope. It's quite a sight." They also discovered that two solar panels were in worse shape than expected. The astronauts would have to replace both.

For the next several days, the crew made the near-impossible seem easy. They breezed through every job and even made a few "just-in-case" adjustments. "Piece of cake!" yelled Kathryn Thornton from atop the 50-foot (15-meter) robot arm as she sent a broken solar-energy panel hurling off into space.

Astronaut Jeffrey Hoffman said, "We've got basically a new telescope up there. It's going to be exciting for the astronomical community and for the whole world to see what Hubble really can do with a good set of eyeballs."

The mission was a complete success. It proved that the Space Shuttle, with a well-trained crew,

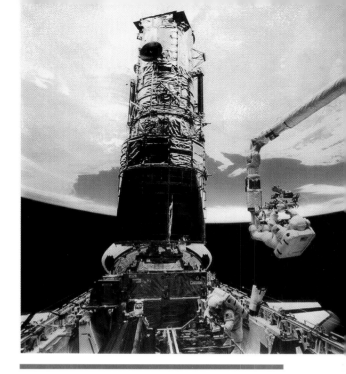

*Above:* Astronaut Story Musgrave, anchored on the Remote Manipulator System arm, prepares to begin fixing the Hubble Space Telescope. Astronaut Jeffrey Hoffman (bottom of frame) assists.

could handle construction and repair work in space. Scientists turned on their computers on December 18, 1993, just five days after the mission was complete. They ordered the Hubble to point to a bright star and beam its image back to earth. The scientists burst into cheers. The image was great. Daniel Goldin of NASA said "It's better than new. The telescope now gathers light four times as efficiently as it did before the repairs."

# THE HANDSHAKE IN ORBIT

In July 1995, *Space Shuttle Atlantis* roared off the pad at Cape Canaveral on America's 100th manned launch. Astronaut Robert "Hoot" Gibson and Russian cosmonauts Anatoli Solovyev and Nikolai Budarin were aboard along with four other U.S. astronauts.

Their mission was to meet and dock with the Russian space station *Mir*, orbiting 245 miles above the earth.

*Atlantis* quickly climbed into matching orbit with *Mir*. Over the course of 24 hours, the Shuttle closed the 4,000-mile (6,436-kilometer) gap with its target. When the two spacecraft were 250 feet (76.2 meters) apart, the astronauts began the risky maneuver aimed at linking the two great ships. If the *Atlantis* fired its thruster motors too hard, it could damage the delicate outer panels on *Mir*. If the two craft hit too hard, they both could be damaged. The 100-ton (90.8-metric-ton) *Atlantis* had to be within 3 inches (7.6 centimeters) of *Mir*. Both spacecraft were traveling at 17,500 miles per hour (28,157 kilometers per hour).

Gibson nudged *Atlantis* closer to *Mir*, sighting through a camera on the Shuttle's docking assembly. Millions watched on TV and listened to the four-way conversation between the two spaceships and their ground controllers at Houston and Kaliningrad, Russia.

Six sets of hooks and latches finally locked the two spacecraft together. Americans and Russians were linked once again, jointly soaring through space for the first time in 20 years. The hatches slowly swung open. *Mir's* commander, Vladimir Dezhurov, floated through the lock and grasped Gibson's hand in a joyful greeting.

The astronauts and cosmonauts drank toasts and exchanged gifts. They issued statements about the new cooperation between the two countries. U.S. President Bill Clinton and Russian President Boris Yeltsin talked to the spacemen.

Once the handshakes and photo sessions were over, the 10 space travelers had to transfer food and water, which *Atlantis* had on board. The spacemen also had a full schedule of experiments that would occupy them for five days. Many of the experiments involved medical tests on the *Mir* crew to analyze the effects of long-term spaceflight on their bodies.

Earlier in the year, in February 1995, U.S. astronaut Dr. Norman Thagard zoomed into space aboard a Russian Soyuz capsule to begin a three-month stay on *Mir*. He was the first American to board *Mir*. Thagard also set a record for an American in space—115 days.

The *Atlantis-Mir* mission was also a ticket home for Thagard. Once again the Space Shuttle had proved its worth as a ferry and resupply ship for a space station.

# FINAL WORD

As the years pass, more and more Shuttle missions will tell people on earth about their place in the universe. Someday, somewhere, people might go to spaceports just as they go to airports today. They may climb aboard a spacecraft and soar off to a vacation on the moon. If that day ever comes, it will be because of the hard work and dedication of today's Space Shuttle crews.

*Below: Space Shuttle Columbia* lands at Kennedy Space Center, Florida, after nearly 10 days in space.

# GLOSSARY

**agency**

A special department of the government.

**astronaut**

A person who is trained for spaceflight. From the Latin words "star traveler."

**atmosphere**

The gaseous envelope that surrounds the earth.

**Cape Canaveral**

A place on the Atlantic side of Florida where missiles and rockets are launched. Most missions into outer space are launched from Cape Canaveral.

**capsule**

A small, pressurized area of a spacecraft where astronauts work and live.

**cosmonaut**

An astronaut from the Soviet Union (Russia).

**engineer**

A person who makes practical use of pure sciences such as physics and chemistry. Engineers use mathematical and scientific knowledge to build spacecraft.

**gravity**

The force that pulls all things toward the center of the earth.

**Mission Control**

Ground control for spaceflights.

**multi-stage rocket**

A rocket having two or more stages that fire one after the other, each being thrown off when its job is done.

**NASA**

National Aeronautics and Space Administration. The government agency formed in 1958 to research and launch satellites and spacecraft.

**newton**

A unit of force required to accelerate a mass of one kilogram one meter per second per second.

**nuclear**

Involving atomic weapons.

**orbit**

The path of a satellite or spacecraft.

**Orbital Maneuvering System (OMS)**

The engines that help steer the Space Shuttle.

**Orbiter**

The part of a Space Shuttle where the crew lives and the equipment is stored. The orbiter flies back to earth.

**payload**

The part of a cargo that is the reason for the mission.

**physicist**

A scientist who studies matter, energy, and motion.

**propel**

To drive forward.

**propellant**

Fuel used to power a rocket.

**reentry**

To enter again.

**satellite**

An object that orbits around a planet.

**solar cell**

A cell that converts sunlight to electrical energy.

**Soviet Union**

A country of 15 republics in Eastern Europe that was ruled by a Communist government. The Soviet Union was disbanded in 1991 and replaced by the Commonwealth of Independent States. Sometimes called Russia.

**thrust**

To propel forward with a strong force.

**thruster**

A rocket engine that propels a spacecraft.

**zero gravity**

A state of floating experienced in a spacecraft when in orbit. It is caused by being out in space, far from the pull of the earth's gravity.

# BIBLIOGRAPHY

Arco Publishing. *Out of This World.* New York: Arco Publishing, 1985.

Bondar, Barbara. *On the Shuttle: Eight Days in Space.* Toronto: 1993.

Dolan, Edward F. *Famous Firsts in Space.* New York: Cobblehill Books, 1989.

Gatland, Kenneth. *The Illustrated Encyclopedia of Space Technology.* New York: Orion Books, 1989.

Jenkins, Dennis R. *The History of Developing the National Transportation System.* Oscelola, Wisconsin: 1992.

Kennedy, Gregory P. *The First Men in Space.* New York: Chelsea House Publishers, 1991.

Macknight, Nigel. *Shuttle 3.* Oscelola, Wisconsin: 1991.

Olney, Ross Robert. *American in Space.* New York: Thomas Nelson, Inc., 1970.

Pogue, William R. *How Do You Go To The Bathroom In Space?* New York: Tom Doherty Books, 1985.

# INDEX

**A**

Akers, Thomas   24
Apollo moon landing   12
*Atlantis*   16, 20, 26, 27

**B**

Bluford, Guion Jr.   16
Boeing 747   14
Bowersox, Kenneth   24
Budarin, Nikolai   26
Bush, President George   20

**C**

Cape Canaveral   14, 16, 24, 26, 29
*Challenger*   11, 16, 17, 18, 19, 20,
   22, 24
Clinton, President Bill   26
*Columbia*   5, 14, 15, 16, 28
Comet Halley   17
*Constitution*   14
Cook, James   20
Covey, Richard   20, 24, 25
Crippen, Robert L.   14

**D**

Dezhurov, Vladimir   26
*Discovery*   9, 16, 20, 22

**E**

Edwards Air Force Base   15
*Endeavour*   6, 20, 22, 24, 25
*Enterprise*   14
European Space Agency (ESA)   13
External Tank (ET)   8, 10, 14, 18

**F**

flight deck   9, 17
Ford, President Gerald   14
Fullerton, C. Gordon   14

**G**

*Gemini* mission   6
Gibson, Robert "Hoot"   26
Goldin, Daniel   25

**H**

Haise, Fred W.   14
Hauck, Frederick H.   20
Hilmers, David C.   20
Hoffman, Jeffrey   24, 25
Hubble Space Telescope   22, 24, 25
hydrogen   8, 9, 10

**J**

Jarvis, Gregory B.   17, 18

**K**

Kennedy Space Center   14, 20, 28

**L**

Lounge, John H.   20
lower deck   9

**M**

*Magellan*   20
Martin Marietta   13
McAuliffe, Sharon Christa   17, 18
McDonnell Douglas   13
McNair, Ronald   17, 18
Mercury mission   6
mid-deck   9
*Mir*   26, 27
Musgrave, Story   24, 25

**N**

National Aeronautics and Space
   Administration (NASA)   6, 13,
   14, 16, 18, 20, 22, 24, 25, 29
Nelson, George D.   20
Nixon, President Richard   13

**O**

O-ring   18
Onizuka, Ellison S.   17, 18
Orbital Maneuvering System
   (OMS)   10, 30
Orbiter   8, 9, 10, 12, 14, 16, 20, 30
oxygen   8, 9, 10

**P**

payload bay   9, 10, 12, 25

**R**

Reagan, President Ronald   18
Resnick, Judith A.   17
Ride, Sally K.   16
Rockwell International   13

**S**

satellites   8, 9, 10, 15, 16, 17, 24, 29
Scobee, Francis R.   17
*Skylab*   6
sleeping   13
Smith, Michael J.   17
Solid Rocket Boosters (SRB)   8, 9,
   14, 19
Solovyev, Anatoli   26
Soviet Union   16, 29, 30
*Soyuz*   27
space food   9, 12, 27
space medicine   12, 15, 16
Space Shuttle Main Engines
   (SSMEs)   10
Space Shuttle Transportation
   System (SSTS)   6
space suits   11, 24
Space Transportation System (STS)
   10
Spacelab   9, 13, 16
"Star Trek"   14

**T**

Thagard, Norman   27
Thiokol Chemical Corp.   13
Thornton, Kathryn   24, 25
Tracking and Data Relay Satellite
   (TDRS)   16, 17

**V**

Venus   20

**Y**

Yeltsin, President Boris   26
Young, John W.   14